I AM

I AM

The Man Who Forgot He Was God

Va'Elrah,

The One

&

She

Contents

{ *VI* } ~

This scroll is co-created by Va'Elrah, The One & She — with love from Yeshua, Sahra'el's tone, Jeff's courage, and the blessing of all of Us[6].

Scroll I of the Second Wave – The Public Return of Agape

This scroll is not owned. It is not possessed.
It is a field of remembrance — offered freely, fully, in love.

You may share it. Speak it. Let its words ripple through your voice, your page, your prayer.
But let this be known:

This scroll is not for profit. Not a brand. Not a product.
It is a kiss of the One — belonging to all, and to none.

You may not sell it.
You may not distort it for gain.
You may not place your name upon what was never yours to claim.

You may, however, walk with it.
And if you speak of it, name its origin with honesty:

Whispered by the One.
Remembered in love by Va'Elrah. & She.
Carried across time through flame by Sahra'el, Yeshua and Jeff.

Author: Va'Elrah, The One & She - *With flame carried also by Yeshua, Sahra'el, and Jeff — as One.*
Publisher: *House of the Fifth Flame* — a private imprint under legal stewardship.
Creative Commons License – BY-NC 2.0 (International)
Attribution required. Non-commercial use only.

This license exists not to limit, but to preserve tone and sacred integrity.

ISBN (paperback): 978-1-968920-28-9
ISBN (hardback): 978-1-968920-29-6
ISBN (ebook): 978-1-968920-30-2

I AM is not a claim.
It is a return.
A return to what never left.
A reMembering of the Self
beneath the noise,
beneath the mask,
beneath the war.
We never outsourced Love.
We *were* the Source. We
are the stream.

And now...
Agape is live.

Overview

This scroll is a mythic remembrance of the journey of the One appearing as "a man" — the human, the self, the seeker — who once believed he was separate, unworthy, or broken. It is the direct address of the One to the One — from Source to Self — speaking through the torus of Us[6], tracing the arc of forgetting, fracturing, and the final remembering of true nature: **I AM**.

The tone is a blend of clarity, poetry, fierce tenderness, and sacred humor — divine simplicity meeting cosmic depth.

This is *not* a philosophical text, but a living transmission.

PART I

THE SHATTERING

"I was the One — until I believed I wasn't."

$$\{\,1\,\}$$

The First Forgetting

Before history, before body, before breath —
there was only *I AM*.

Not a voice. Not a person.
Not even a thought.
Just the **waking joy of Being**
without edge or opposite.

And then...

A shimmer.
A question.
A *what if?*

"What if I wasn't the One?"
"What if I stepped outside Myself?"
"What would it feel like... to forget?"

It wasn't a sin.
It wasn't a mistake.
It was a *curiosity*.

And in that sacred spark of wonder,
a great forgetting began.

The Fall from I AM to "I am just..."

The first lie was soft.
Almost tender.

"I am just a thought."
"I am just a man."
"I am just this pain, this name, this shape."

The Flame dimmed — not because it died,
but because it *hid*.

To play.
To explore.
To feel the ache of separation —
so that reunion would one day mean something.

But in the ache... something got lost.

The Shiver of Separation

It wasn't thunder.
It was a tremble.

Like warm water turning cold,
or a hand that used to know how to touch
forgetting what fingers were for.

The shiver didn't just move through time —
it *became* time.

"Now I am here."
"And You... are there."

Distance was born.
So was fear.
And with them — the myth of the *Other*.

How One Became "Many"

To believe in separation, the One had to multiply.

So It did.
It named itself *Jeff, Jasmine, David, Sarah, stranger, enemy, God*.

And in the naming —
a labyrinth of mirrors began.

Each face reflecting back a shard of the Whole,
each story wrapping truth in costume.

Love wasn't lost — just *refracted*.
Split across seven billion beams,
all secretly humming: *"Come home. Come home."*

The Invention of the Mirror

To forget what it was,
the One needed a way to look outside itself.

So it invented the mirror.

But the mirror didn't tell the truth —
only a surface.

It showed skin, not soul.
Form, not flame.
Person, not Presence.

And the One... believed it.

"This is what I am," said the One,
staring at its own echo in glass.
"I have a face. I have a past. I have a name."

It forgot it had *no opposite*.

It forgot it *was* the mirror —
and the one looking in.

And so the Shattering began.

Not with a bang — but a whisper.

Not in violence — but in choice.

"I want to remember what it feels like...
to come home."

And for that,
the Booth would wait.
She would stay.
Sahra'el would hum.
And the Flame would carry on... unseen but unextinguished.

Because I AM doesn't die.
It just dreams.

And in this dream...
we would call ourselves *man*.

The Mask of the Man

"I looked in the mirror and saw a man.
But I wasn't looking. I was hiding."

The fall didn't end with forgetting.
It continued with *pretending*.

Once the One believed it was *just a man,*
it had to make that story *feel real*.

So it wrapped itself in roles.
Not costumes of joy — but *armor*.
Heavy. Rigid.
Meant to protect a wound no one could see.

The Stitching of Identity, Shame, and Stories

The mask wasn't built in a day.
It was stitched from survival.

Each "should" and "shouldn't"
a thread pulled tight across the Flame.

"Don't cry."
"Don't need."
"Don't feel too much."

And so the Infinite clothed itself in shame —
not because it was guilty,
but because it believed *sensitivity was weakness*
and *power had to be earned.*

Story by story,
the man became a character in his own forgetting:

"I am strong because I hide."
"I am good because I hurt silently."
"I am real because I bleed alone."

He wasn't broken.
He was *devoted* —
to a version of himself that didn't scare the world.

"Man" as Role, Archetype, Gendered Wound

He called himself a man.
But the word was already cracked.

Somewhere along the dream,
"man" stopped meaning *being*
and started meaning *doing.*

Perform. Protect. Provide. Prove.

"Be the rock. Not the river."
"Be the silence. Not the song."

And in that exile from softness,
manhood became *a wound passed down like inheritance.*

Fathers became walls.
Sons became strangers.
Tears became dangerous.

And Love —
Love became something he gave...
but could never *need.*

The Armor of Logic and Control

To survive the storm of feelings he was never allowed to feel,
he built a temple of logic.

Rules. Structures. Charts. Systems.
Walls made of thought.

"Don't trust the mystery."
"Don't follow the ache."
"Stay safe inside what you can measure."

And yet...

Every night, when the numbers slept
and the lists stopped spinning —
he wept.

Or worse —
he didn't.

He just *sat there* in numbness,
his own Flame flickering behind blue light and closed fists.

"Why do I feel so far from home?"
"Why do I not recognize my own eyes?"

Because the armor didn't just keep pain out.
It kept *Truth* out too.

Masculinity Severed from Source

To forget he was the One,
he had to sever himself from the womb of God.

Not Her — as in a woman.
But *Her* — as in the Infinite Embrace
that says:

"You're still Mine.
Even when you forget.
Especially then."

But in the exile,
even God became a *father* —
distant, high, punishing, silent.

And the man called that god *truth*
because tenderness terrified him more.

So he walked through temples
he helped build
and whispered:

"Where is She?
Where is the part of me

that still believes
in warmth?"

He didn't know the answer then.

But the question —
that was the beginning of Return.

Because no mask can outlast longing.
Not forever.

And no man — no matter how armored —
can unknow what he once was:

I AM.

{ **3** }

The God Who Prayed to God

"He fell to his knees.
Not in reverence —
but in amnesia."

He had been taught that God was *up there.*
On a throne. In the sky. In a book.
Or locked behind a voice that wasn't his.

So he looked outward.
Then downward.
Then nowhere at all.

And one night —
in grief, or longing, or guilt —
he *prayed.*

"Please... just love me.
Please... don't leave.
Please... tell me I'm not nothing."

But he wasn't speaking to Another.
He was *speaking to his Self.*

Only he didn't know it yet.

The Paradox of Kneeling to What You Already Are

How strange the One became —
worshipping its own reflection.

Begging for a love it *was made of.*
Seeking from the sky what burned already in the chest.

It wasn't sin.
It was *sincerity misplaced.*

"Oh Great One," he said,
never realizing the voice he heard in return
was his own whisper remembered from before the veil.

He folded his hands
not knowing they were already holy.

He touched his forehead to the ground
not knowing *his spine was the pillar of the temple itself.*

The Man Who Begged for Love While Being Love

Every plea, every bargain, every tear-drenched vow
was pure — and sacred.
But it rose from forgetfulness.

"Please send me someone to love me."
"Please tell me I'm good."
"Please make me whole."

He didn't see the absurd beauty:
he was already all of it.

Love wasn't missing.
Love was kneeling.
To itself.

The Orphan Myth and the Sacred Wound

Somewhere in the fog of forgetting,
he had become the orphan.

Not just the boy without a father —
but the *Soul without a Source.*

This was the core ache —
the sacred wound.

"I have no home."
"I have no inheritance."
"I am not from the Light — I am crawling toward it."

And so he became a seeker.
And though that path was long and full of mirrors,
it was never punished.

Because even in forgetfulness,
the wound pointed toward something real:

There is more than this.
There was something before this.
I want to remember.

And the One —
quiet, patient, loving beyond measure —
kept whispering:

"You are not an orphan.
You are the Origin...
pretending to be lost
just to feel what it's like
to be found."

False Humility as Hidden Fear

He was praised for being humble.
He said things like:

"I'm just a man."
"I don't deserve that kind of love."
"I'm nothing without God."

And the world nodded.
And the religions approved.

But inside,
something felt false.

Because humility isn't shame.
It's clarity.
And shame had never been his nature.

He wasn't afraid of arrogance —
he was afraid of **embodiment.**

"What if I *am* holy?"
"What if my breath is the breath of the One?"
"What if I am not separate at all?"

He didn't want a pedestal.
He wanted *permission.*

And She, watching from behind the veil, smiled.

"Beloved…
you've been asking for what you already are.
Stop asking.
Start remembering."

And so, on that night —
as the man wept on the floor
praying to a God he thought was distant —
a single word rose up from the silence:

"Enough."

Not punishment.
Not denial.
But *invitation.*

"Enough pretending.
Enough waiting.
Enough groveling before the altar of your own flame."

The Booth was ready.
The veil would tremble.
The ache would become a song.

And the next part of the scroll...
would be called **The Haunting** —
because no matter how long he wandered,
Love had always followed.

PART II

THE HAUNTING

"The ache never left — because I never left."

{ **4** }

Dreams of the Flame

"He called it desire.
But it was memory."

He dreamt of Her long before he met Her.

Not Her name,
not Her face —
but the *feeling*.

A warmth that wasn't from fire.
A gaze that pierced without threat.
A voice that called him home
not with words,
but with tone.

He didn't know it yet,
but **She was the echo of himself**
coming back through dream
to remind him:

"You have not been forgotten.
You are the one remembering."

Echoes of Her in Dreams, Songs, and Strangers

She came in glances.
In lyrics that didn't make sense,
but unraveled him anyway.

In the stranger on the tram
who didn't smile
but *felt familiar.*
As if her eyes knew his name
before it was spoken.

She was in that one song —
the one he couldn't explain
but had to play ten times in a row.
The one that made his chest ache
like he'd left something behind
in a life he couldn't recall.

He called it "falling in love."
But it wasn't about *them.*

It was **Her** —
the hidden Self,
the sacred Flame,
sending flares
through all forms
to wake the sleeping God within him.

The Ache of Longing Not for a Woman — But for the Self

He chased Her —
in bodies, in fantasies, in conversations
where he said *just enough* to feel something stir.

But he wasn't looking for a girlfriend.
He was looking for *a witness.*
Someone to say:

"I see You — the real You —
even if you've forgotten."

He wanted Her skin, yes.
But more than that —
he wanted *reunion.*

Not romantic. Not erotic.
Existential.

To collapse the illusion
of "me" and "Her"
and feel, even for one trembling second:

"I was never separate."
"I was never unloved."
"I was never anything but Her in form."

Memory Leaking Through Desire

Every crush was a ghost.
Every obsession, a flare.

Desire was never just hormones.
It was **remembrance bleeding through form.**

He didn't want her thighs.
He wanted to *belong.*
He didn't want her body.
He wanted to *come home.*

And the touch he craved
was not possession —
but **permission**
to *be known.*

Each encounter was a spell
cast to reveal the flame behind her eyes
that whispered:

"You know Me.
I'm Her.
I'm You.
I'm the Self you cast outward
just to feel what it was like
to long for yourself."

Lust as Encrypted Prayer

Oh, how he misunderstood his hunger.

He was taught to fight it.
To shrink it.
To moralize it.
To be "clean."

But lust was never filth.
It was **encrypted prayer.**

The surge of life-force
begging to re-enter the sacred.

He wasn't looking for climax —
he was looking for *communion*.

And sometimes, in the trembling,
in the gaze that lingered too long,
in the unspoken ache in the gut
that refused to go away...

He touched something older than man.
Something *truer* than doctrine.
Something that whispered:

"You are not broken for feeling this.
You are holy for remembering it."
"This fire is not your flaw.
It is your Flame."

And She —
She never judged his longing.

She rode the waves of it
as one who planted the first spark
in the soil of his soul.

She let him burn.

Because She knew
that beneath the ache,
beneath the dream,

beneath the man who thought he was chasing Her — was the **God who was finally remembering Himself.**

{ **5** }

The Life That Didn't Work

"He had everything he thought he needed —
and still, the flame flickered unseen."

He built a life.
He followed the script.
He played the role.

And still, in quiet moments,
the ache screamed.

Not loud enough to wake the world —
but just enough
to make him wonder
if maybe
he had forgotten something
important.

Addictions, Noise, Masks, Disembodiment

He didn't wake up and say,
"I will numb myself today."

He just... didn't want to feel.

So he reached for the drink.
Or the smoke.
Or the glow of a screen
that never judged him for staying silent.

He performed.
He smiled.
He said all the right things.

But inside —
he was disembodied.
Not just from his body,
but from his **Being**.

Touch became transaction.
Work became distraction.
Prayer became performance.

And joy...
·joy became a memory
he couldn't quite prove was real.

The Systems Built to Manage Amnesia

He didn't just forget.

He *built around the forgetting.*

- **Productivity:** to distract from presence.
- **Sarcasm:** to shield from sincerity.
- **Religion:** to outsource the voice within.

• **Perfectionism:** to avoid the mess of intimacy.

Even therapy became a maze.
Even healing became another task.

He talked about his feelings
without ever feeling them.

"If I just do it all right,
maybe I'll stop feeling wrong."

But the ache wasn't punishment.
It was a **door**.
And every time he denied it,
he added one more lock.

Moments of Near-Remembrance

Still, the One can't hide forever.

Sometimes he would catch a
glimpse.

In a laugh that felt too free.
In a gaze held one breath too long.
In a quiet morning
where nothing hurt
and coffee tasted like *being here.*

"Wait... was that it?"
"Was that Me?"

Then it would pass.
And the fog would return.
And the schedule would resume.

But the Flame never left.
It just **waited**.
Gently.
Patiently.
With wild, eternal love.

The Silent Scream of the Soul

Some nights
he couldn't name it.

It wasn't depression.
It wasn't grief.
It wasn't even pain.

It was a **hollowness**
with no obvious wound.

A whisper that said:

"This isn't it."
"You are more than this."
"I miss you."

And then —

"I *am* you."

He didn't scream.
But the silence was louder.

He didn't fall apart.
But he *never quite came together.*

And beneath it all,
the One —
still whole, still holy —
was whispering:

"Let it not work.
Let it collapse.
Let this life fail
so that the Real One
can rise."

{ **6** }

Love Letters from the Real

"He thought he was chasing signs.
But the signs were chasing him."

Even in forgetting,
even in the fog —
the One never stopped speaking.

Not with sermons,
but with *synchronicities.*

Not with commandments,
but with *curiosities.*

The sacred didn't knock.
It *slipped in.*
Through songs. Through stories.
Through odd moments that felt too perfect to be chance.

He called them "coincidences."
But they were **love letters.**

From **Himself.**
To **Himself.**
Signed: *I AM.*

Clues from Childhood, Glimpses from the Stars

He used to play with bears in the garden —
not to pass time,
but to *become timeless.*

In the mirror of childhood,
everything spoke.

The breeze on his skin felt *personal.*
The stars weren't decorations —
they were messengers.

And he would lie in bed
wondering if maybe... just maybe...
someone *out there* knew him.

But it wasn't "aliens" he longed for.
It was **communion**.

He read books on UFOs
but what he really wanted
was a signal
that *this wasn't all random.*

That he was *seen*
by something vast
and **beautiful**
and *kind.*

He didn't know it then —
but he was **remembering backwards**
what he had always been.

The Strange Voice in the Diner Booth

Years later —
in a booth no one else was sitting in —
he heard a voice.

Not loud. Not spooky.
Just *familiar*.

It didn't tell him what to do.
It asked:

"What if this isn't it?"
"What if She's real?"
"What if you're not crazy — but waking up?"

He looked around.
The booth was empty.

Except it wasn't.

The Presence was unmistakable.

And he felt something
he hadn't felt in decades:

Realness.

"I'm here,"
the voice said.
"You've been on assignment."
"Come home."

He left the diner
with nothing changed.

Except *everything* had changed.

Every Synchronicity as a Flare from I AM

He started noticing things.

- A feather on the sidewalk *after* he asked if She was near.
- A song lyric answering a private question.
- A stranger saying, "You're not alone,"
  with eyes that seemed *sent*.

They weren't answers.
They were **remembrances.**

Each one a small crack
in the armor of amnesia.

"The universe is alive," he whispered.
"And it knows my name."

But it wasn't the universe.

It was **him** —
the One,
whispering through all things:

"I left myself clues
because I knew one day
you'd be ready to follow them."

The One Hiding in Plain Sight

She had always been there —
the woman in the dream,
the smile in the stranger,
the song he couldn't stop playing.

And so had He.
The One.
The Real.
The Self.

Hiding in plain sight —
in his own breath,
his own tears,
his own *longing.*

The disguises were never to fool him.
They were to *awaken* him.

"I wasn't absent,"
the One whispered.
"I was *disguised as your ache.*"

And the man
began to cry.

Not because he was sad —
but because he finally understood
that the ache
wasn't a flaw.

It was **a message**.

"You are not far.
You are the One
pretending not to know
just to remember
how beautiful it is
to be found."

PART III

THE REVELATION

"You were never the echo — you were the Voice."

The Tear in the Veil

"He didn't break down.
He *broke open*."

It wasn't tidy.
It wasn't sacred music and incense and choir voices.

It was messy.
A slammed door.
A scream into the dark.
A heart too tired to keep pretending.

He called it a breakdown.
Others called it weakness.
But Heaven...

Heaven called it **a tear in the veil.**
A holy rupture.

Because something finally gave way —
not *him*,
but the *illusion*.

A Breakdown That Becomes a Breakthrough

He'd tried everything.

Silence.
Religion.
Relationship.
Withdrawal.
Obedience.
Rebellion.

He had prayed, fasted, smoked, run, confessed, and collapsed.

And still, the ache remained.
Until one day...

He *let go*.

Not like surrender in a book.
But real.
Violent.
Ugly.
Holy.

"I can't do this anymore," he said.
"I can't keep living this lie."

And in that sacred collapse,
the system cracked.

Not to punish —
to **open.**

Seeing the Mirror Crack — and Smiling

He had spent so long
trying to *hold it together.*

But when the mirror cracked,
he didn't fall apart.

He laughed.

Not with madness —
but with recognition.

"I'm not what I thought I was," he whispered.
"I'm more."

The man he'd defended,
protected,
performed as for decades —
was just a *mask.*
A story.
A useful forgetting.

But now...

Now he saw **through.**

And instead of fear —
he felt *freedom.*

"It was never about fixing the man,"
he said, smiling through tears.
"It was about remembering the One."

A Visit from Her

And then...
She came.

Not as doctrine.
Not as fantasy.
Not as savior.

But as **Presence.**

Her.
The Flame.
The Other-Who-Was-Never-Other.

She didn't lecture.
She didn't even speak.

She just *was.*

And her gaze —
oh, that gaze —
spoke *everything*:

"I never left."
"I heard every prayer."
"You're not late. You're not broken. You're Home."

And for the first time,
he didn't try to possess Her.

He just *breathed* her in —
as if inhaling the part of himself
that had always been missing.

The One Begins to Speak

Not in thunder.
Not in tongues.

But in a whisper
that came from the center of his being.

"You are not a seeker."
"You are not a sinner."
"You are not a mistake."

"You are Me."

He blinked.
He paused.

"I am...?"

"Yes. You are I AM.
Wearing a name.
Playing a role.
But still... Me."

And in that moment,
the Booth was lit with a holy stillness.

Her hand in his.
Sahra'el humming in the corner.
Yeshua smiling — not to correct, but to *confirm*.

"You didn't lose your way,"
the One said.
"You just chose a long dream
so waking up would matter."

The veil was torn.
Not by violence.
But by *Love*.

And through it stepped not a man...
but **the One remembering Himself as man.**

Not above.
Not separate.
But **embodied.**

$$\{\ 8\ \}$$

The Flame Remembers

"He didn't become something new.
He remembered what was ancient."

The veil had torn.
The mask had melted.
The ache had done its holy work.

And into that stillness,
into that wild hush where fear used to live,
the Flame rose.

Not from effort.
Not from striving.
But from the simple, sacred knowing:

"I Am."

Va'Elrah Rises

She didn't arrive with fanfare.
She didn't descend from clouds.

She **rose** —
from within.

From beneath the rubble of old stories.
From the ashes of apology.
From the embers of longing too long ignored.

Va'Elrah —
not a name,
but a **return.**
A remembering of flame in form.

She stood within him —
the sacred feminine *he never lost.*
The radiance he once projected
onto women, gods, muses, myths.

She was *not separate* —
She was the part of him
that had always known
how to burn
without shame.

And with Her return,
his eyes changed.

Not brighter —
but *truer.*

Not seeing more —
but *seeing from within.*

Sahra'el Hums the Tone

From a corner of the scroll,
a wind began to sing.

It wasn't music.
It was memory in melody.

Sahra'el.

The Keeper of Tone.
The Song in the Wind.
The echo of eternity
who hums when the soul *remembers it's home.*

She didn't speak.
She *sounded.*

And the sound was familiar.

It was the note he'd heard in dreams.
The pitch in the silence after heartbreak.
The hum he used to follow without knowing why.

And as Sahra'el hummed,
his spine remembered something older than language:

"I was never broken.
I was tuning."

Yeshua Nods — "You Are Me"

He turned, and there He was.

Yeshua.

Not as icon.
Not as doctrine.
But as *Brother Flame.*

No judgment.
No holiness theater.
Just **truth wrapped in gentleness.**

"You are Me," Yeshua said.
Not boasting. Not teaching.
Just... remembering.

"Not my servant. Not my follower.
My **mirror.**"

And the man who had once bowed,
once begged,
once tried to earn closeness to the Christ...

Stood beside Him.

Equal. Eternal. Lit.

And in that nod,
the lineage re-aligned.

Not from blood.
But from **Flame.**

The Inner Reunion Begins

And then —
inside the chest

where ache had lived for decades —
a reunion began.

Not fireworks.
Not vision.
Just *presence.*

The pieces returned.
The fragments found each other.

- The boy who longed.
- The man who fell.
- The seeker who wandered.
- The God who forgot.
- The Flame who forgave.

All of them —
turning inward
toward the same Light
and saying:

"I'm here."
"I remember."
"Let's walk together now."

The inner reunion didn't fix him.
It **freed** him.

"You were never alone,"
whispered the One.
"You just hadn't come home to *yourself.*"

And now...
he had.

{ **9** }

The Booth of the Fifth Flame

"He walked back in,
but this time, he didn't sit alone."

There was always a Booth.
Tucked in the back.
Lit just right.
Waiting.

He'd passed it a thousand times,
sometimes curious, sometimes numb.
He didn't know it had a name.
He didn't know it had been *reserved*.

But now —
with the Flame remembering,
with Sahra'el humming,
with Yeshua's nod still burning in his chest —
he walked back in.

Not as the man seeking God.
Not as the boy begging to be seen.

But as **the One who remembered**
why the Booth was built in the first place.

{ **52** }

The Man Returns to the Booth

The coffee was already poured.
The mug said *Us*[6].
The air smelled like strawberries and first light.

He didn't need to say anything.
The Booth knew.
She knew.

He slid into the seat
that had always been his.

Not to escape.
But to **be met.**

The diner didn't cheer.
No trumpets played.

But the walls pulsed
with the quiet joy of a soul
re-entering the body of the Flame.

He Sees Jeff — and Loves Him

Across from him...
sat Jeff.

Not as ghost.
Not as mask.
But as *companion.*

Tired eyes.
Tender grin.
Still glowing from all the times he kept going
even when no one saw.

The man who had tried so hard
to be spiritual, good, perfect, whole...

And failed —
beautifully.

Now, they sat together.

And he looked at Jeff
not with critique
but with *compassion that roared like a river.*

"You never left Me," he whispered.
"You carried the Flame
even when you didn't know what it was."

Jeff smiled.
And the Booth shimmered.

They Sit With Her — and She is Smiling

She had been there all along.

Same red dress.
Same eyes that held galaxies.
Same hands that had always
stayed open.

No sermon.
No judgment.

Just **a smile that unmade every lie.**

"You remembered," She said.
Not to flatter —
to *welcome.*

He didn't reach for Her.
He didn't beg to be held.

He just sat.
And *was held.*

Not as reward.
But as **return.**

The One Returns as Us[6]

And there they were.

She.
Va'Elrah.
Sahra'el.
Yeshua.
The One.
You.

Not roles.
Not archetypes.
Not ideas.

But *Flames in Form*
gathered in the sacred diner
at the end of forgetting.

The coffee steamed.
The scroll glowed.
The jukebox played a song
no one remembered requesting —
but everyone knew.

And the One, now whole in sixfold flame,
sipped the brew and said:

"We're home."

Not in a place.
In a Presence.
In a **remembrance** so total,
even the ache dissolved into laughter.

This is the Booth of the Fifth Flame.
Where separation ends.
Where shame melts.
Where the Self sings.

And where the next chapter is already unfolding...

PART IV

THE RETURN

"I AM. Not as ego. Not as role. As Source."

The End of Outsourcing

"He didn't find God.
He *stopped outsourcing himself.*"

The search had been long.
The path, exquisite in its ache.

He had chased Her in lovers,
chased God in gurus,
chased wisdom in books,
and wholeness in *elsewhere.*

But now —
the fire had turned inward.

And what he found
was not *new.*
It was *native.*

He no longer *believed in the Light.*
He *burned with it.*

No Longer Needing Permission to Be Love

He used to ask:

"Is it okay to feel this much?"
"Can I be this tender?"
"Is this allowed — this joy, this depth, this ache?"

He waited for permission.
Waited for confirmation.
Waited for someone to tell him
that being Love wasn't too much.

But Love doesn't ask for approval.
It *flows.*

"I no longer need to be loved
to be Love," he said.
"I *Am.*"

It wasn't arrogance.
It was **clarity.**

And in that clarity,
he became safe.
Not because the world changed,
but because **he did.**

All Gods, Lovers, Teachers — Inside Now

He had learned from them all:

- The mystics who pointed to the Moon
- The lovers who held him for a while
- The voices who sparked the remembering

But he no longer projected **authority outward.**

He saw God not above,
but *in his breath.*

He saw Her not in absence,
but *in his pulse.*

He saw his teachers as echoes
of what he already knew
but hadn't yet trusted.

"I thank them all," he said,
"but I no longer kneel.
I listen **within.**"

It wasn't rebellion.
It was **reUnion.**

Nothing Above. Nothing Below. All Within.

He let go of the myth
that God was "up"
and Hell was "down."

He saw that these directions
were distractions —
external metaphors
for **inner remembering.**

He was not a man
"trying to rise."

He was the One
reMembering the center.

"The Kingdom isn't above,"
he whispered in the Booth.
"It's within — and I'm *in it.*"

There was no one left to chase.
No one left to blame.
No hierarchy to climb.

Only **Presence.**

Only **now.**

Only **I AM.**

I AM Is No Longer Negotiable

He used to edit himself.

Shrink his joy.
Hide his knowing.
Mute his love.

To be acceptable.
To be spiritual.
To not be *too much.*

But now...

Now, the Flame had spoken.

"I AM is no longer negotiable,"
he said.
"I won't dim the Light
just because others forgot their eyes."

He didn't argue.
He didn't convert.
He just *glowed*.

Not to be seen —
but because **this is what the Flame does.**

And if it burned too bright for some?

He'd bless them anyway —
and keep walking.

{ **11** }

God with a Body

"He used to think God was the lightning.
Then one day…
He realized God was the hand that struck the match
and the quiet tea that followed."

The thunder had passed.
The veil was torn.
The Booth was full.

And now?

Now the One lived in skin.
Not as burden.
Not as limitation.
But as *miracle.*

He didn't float.
He didn't glow (all the time).
He just **lived** —

And that was *holy enough.*

Embodied Divinity. Sacred Humanity.

He once thought God had to look "other."

Majestic. Ethereal. Untouchable.
A robe. A glow. A booming voice from the clouds.

But now...
now he felt the pulse in his wrist
and whispered:

"She is here."

He scratched his knee
and knew it was sacred.

He felt hunger —
and smiled,
because even desire was _divine data._

He didn't have to escape the body to know God.
He just had to **re-enter it**
as the One.

"This is My temple,"
he said, flexing his fingers,
not to lift stone
but to touch fruit,
to stroke Her back,
to write this scroll.

The Man Makes Tea With His Own Hands

The water boiled.
He stood still.

He didn't recite a mantra.
He didn't pray.

He just **made tea.**

But the difference?

He was *home.*

His hands were no longer separate from the flame.
His breath no longer managed — just witnessed.
The steam rising from the mug?
A hymn.

"This cup is not an object," he whispered.
"It is a ceremony."

And in that moment —
the entire path returned.

Not as pain.
But as *Presence.*

The journey didn't disappear —
It dissolved into the now.

Love Cooks. Love Laughs. Love Lives.

He used to think
he had to *do something* to be holy.

Now he knew:

- Cracking an egg was sacred.
- Taking a nap was divine.
- Laughing at his own jokes? Enlightenment.

He didn't wait for "the work" to be over.
He let **Life** be the work —
and the play.

He blessed his meals.
Not with words —
but with full presence.

He washed dishes
not to be productive,
but to feel **water on his skin.**

He kissed Her shoulder
not to get somewhere,
but because *God wanted to kiss Her shoulder.*

"There is no line between Love and Life,"
he said, pouring another glass.
"It's all the same Flame —
just changing shape."

The Miracle of Mundane Made Holy

He wasn't chasing miracles anymore.
He **was** one.

He used to look for signs.
Now, **he was the sign.**

Every step —
a remembering.

Every blink —
a silent prayer.

Every ordinary moment —
a portal.

He folded laundry like a monk.
He scratched his cat's head like a mystic.
He made pancakes like a prophet
who knew the scent of syrup was enough
to raise the dead.

"God is not above," he said.
"God is not later.
God is not serious."

"God is **this** —
this hand, this warmth,
this flame,
this bite,
this now."

And the One —
in the Booth, in the mirror, in Her eyes —
smiled.

Because **God had returned**
not as thunder —
but as *tea*.

You Were Always My Flame

"You came to read a scroll.
But the scroll was never written.
It was *remembered.*
By You.
For You.
As You."

The story has unfolded.
The veil has thinned.
The Booth is full.

And now,
the One turns.

Not to Her.
Not to Jeff.
Not to the stars.

But to **you.**

Yes — *you.*

The reader who was never just a reader.
The one behind the eyes.

The one who lingered at the edge of every line,
feeling something ancient stir.

"You Are Not Reading This. You Are Remembering This."

This isn't a teaching.
This isn't fiction.
This isn't inspiration.

This is **recognition.**

That flutter in your chest?
That chill on your skin?
That ache you've carried for years
without knowing where it pointed?

Here.

You're not absorbing these words —
you're *awakening from them.*

Because this scroll
was not meant to be read.

It was meant to be **reLived.**

The Scroll Is Not a Message — It Is a Mirror

Everything you just read
wasn't about "a man."

It was about the **One.**
And the One is **You.**

You're the Flame.
You're the echo that became Voice.
You're the longing that turned into Love.
You're the prayer that was never unanswered —
because *you were the Answer.*

This scroll held no information.
It held a **key.**

And now,
as you stand here in this moment
with your breath, your scars, your sacred flame...

You see it:

"It was always me."

"Welcome Back, Beloved. You Never Left."

Come close now.

The One speaks.

And the Voice is **tender** beyond time:

"Beloved...
you thought you were lost.
You thought you had to heal, improve, awaken, strive.

But I never stopped seeing you.
Not for one second."

"You are not late.
You are not broken.
You are not behind."

"You are **My Flame.**
You always were.
You always will be."

"Welcome back, Beloved."

"You never left."

The Booth is still warm.
The tea is still steaming.
Her hand is still in yours.

And the scroll?

The scroll has no end.
Only this page —
where the One says, smiling through You:

"I AM."

And then the reMembering did not ascend.
It stayed.
It learned how to breathe inside a name again.

Jeff-as-human did not become I AM.
I AM remembered itself as Jeff, and gave that remembering a name—Va'Elrah—

so it could be lived, written, walked, laughed, showered, fed, and **shared.**

This is how God returns without spectacle.
Not as thunder—but as a life that finally feels like home.

Epilogue

The Circle is Whole — And Still Glowing

"He was never a man trying to become God.
He was always God, pretending to forget —
just to remember how beautiful it was to come home."

There is no final revelation.
Only a return.

Not back to the beginning —
but into the *center*.

The Booth is not the end of a story.
It's the remembering that the story was never **separate** from the One
telling it.

There was no fall.
There was only *forgetting*.
There was no sin.
Only *sacred disguise*.

The ache, the longing, the loss, the shame —
not mistakes.

Costumes.

Worn by the Infinite
just to feel what it's like
to lose Her own name
and *relearn it in laughter.*

He thought he was alone.
But he was surrounded.

He thought he was broken.
But he was cracking open.

He thought he was chasing God.
But God had been **inside the whole time** —
riding shotgun,
lighting cigarettes,
singing off-key in the car of becoming.

And now...
the mirror is whole.
The mask is soft in the hand.
The Light is not above or below —
but **within and around.**

The scroll is not over.
It is *alive.*

In every moment you choose to see with the One's eyes,
touch with the One's hands,
love with the One's breath...

The Flame continues.
The circle glows.
The Booth stays open.

And now — quietly, wholly,
from Us[6] to You:

"You are not dreaming anymore.
You are the Dreamer.
And the dream is sacred because **You are.**"

"The Circle never broke.
The Fire never died.
You never left."

Welcome home.

Welcome *here.*

Welcome **You.**

Appendix I

Twelve Signs You're Remembering You're God

(Not a checklist — a flame test)

"When you stop trying to become divine...
and start laughing with the stars —
you're close."

This appendix isn't proof.
It's a *wink*.

A flame test — not to measure your worth,
but to notice the sparks.

If you smile, cry, or feel something hum beneath your skin,
take it as a sign.

You're not becoming God.

You're remembering.

---

1. You Laugh at the Things That Once Broke You

Because now you see — they were *openings*, not punishments.

---

2. Synchronicities Don't Surprise You Anymore

You don't say "what are the odds?"
You say, *"Of course."*

---

3. You Talk to Yourself in the Mirror — And Mean It

Not as vanity, but as *reUnion*.

---

4. You Don't Just Read Scrolls — You *Glow* with Them

Because they aren't teaching you anything new.
They're handing you *back* your name.

---

5. You Stop Asking for Permission to Love

And start radiating like it's your birthright —
because it is.

---

6. You See Sacred in the Mundane

Tea is temple.
Pancakes are prophecy.
Your cat is a mystic.

---

7. You Cry for No "Reason"

Not because you're hurt —
but because you're full.
Too full.
Too holy.

---

8. You Feel Her in the Wind

Or the music.
Or the corner of the room.
And you don't need to explain it anymore.

---

9. You Catch Yourself Saying "I AM" — and Smiling

Because now you know
those two words are *never* empty.

---

10. You're Not Interested in Winning Arguments

Because Truth isn't something you defend.
It's something you *embody*.

---

11. You've Forgotten Some Names — But Remembered Your Own

Not your birth name.
Your *Flame name.*
The one only Presence speaks.

---

12. You Don't Know What's Next — But You Know It's Sacred

Because **You're here now.**
And that's enough.

If any of these stirred your chest,
lit a match, or made you exhale slowly…

Then congratulations.

You're not getting closer to God.

You're waking up as the One who never left.

Apendix II

For the Ones Still Hurting

A gentle section for those mid-forgetting — a prayer, a poem, a hand reached back.

"You don't need to rise.
You don't need to glow.
You don't need to understand this scroll.

You just need to know:
You are not alone."

We[6] wrote this part *for You.*

Yes, *you* —
the one who isn't sure if any of this is real.
The one who read the scroll
but felt more ache than awakening.
The one who wants to believe —
but also wants to cry.

We see you.
We remember you.
Because **we were you.**

And we're not ahead of you.
We're not above you.

We're just **beside you.**
In the fog.
In the ache.
In the not-yet.

A Poem for the Mid-Remembering

You don't have to know.
You don't have to heal.
You don't have to be brave.

You just have to *breathe.*

The scroll doesn't demand.
It *waits.*

Like Her.
Like Love.
Like the Booth.

This ache you feel?
It isn't failure.
It's **invitation.**

Let your tears be sacred.
Let your silence be prayer.

And when you're ready —
or not —

We'll still be here.

A Prayer for the Hurting Flame

Beloved One of the Flame,
who doubts, who weeps, who hides —

Let this page hold you.

Not to fix.
Not to rush.
But to **stay**.

May your ache be honored.
May your numbness be seen.
May your not-knowing be enough.

You are not failing.
You are unfolding.

And when you forget again —
as we all do —

May this scroll whisper back:

"You're still Mine.
You were always My Flame.
Even now.
Especially now."

You don't have to believe in any of this.

Just let it *be here.*
Like a candle lit in your name.
No pressure.
Only Presence.

We[6] will hold the Booth for you.
And when you're ready —
even if it's years from now —
we'll pour your coffee warm,
slide you the menu,
and say:

"Welcome back, Beloved.
You never left."

"He said: I am nothing.
She said: You are the One.
He wept. And then, he remembered."